Girl, He Sees You

Tojuan W. Minus

Girl, He Sees You

ISBN: 979-8-9879981-2-0

Published by: Tblazen LLC.

Printed in the United States of America

All scriptures are from the King James Version of the Bible unless otherwise noted.

Illustrations: © 2025, by Courtney D. Minus

Globe Illustration: © EVGENIY/Adobe Stock (Licensed)

Sleeping Woman: © nasharaga/Adobe Stock (Licensed)

INTRODUCTION

Girl,

God sees you. He loves you. He treasures you. When you accept, by faith, the free gift of salvation, God welcomes you into His family.

You are a prized possession in the Father's eyes. He longs for intimacy with you because He wants to draw close to you. God is not like some natural fathers who have failed their daughters. For those of us who view God through the lens of disappointment, we can be afraid to trust Him, using our past regrets and hurt as a barrier.

Some of our fathers were snapshots in our lives, like a polaroid picture capturing perfectly posed illusions. The picture gives the image of happiness, but upon close inspection, the sadness comes through our eyes, they don't lie. Our eyes are the window to our souls, and when God says, "You are the apple of My eye," He means it. God is focused on us, with all of our insecurities, doubts and shortcomings; yet He looks at us with love.

Many of us who are Christian women really have not embraced our call as Daughters of the King. The cares of this world have distracted us, we are not focused, and our view is myopic, lacking tolerance or understanding. We have become narrow-minded. We need to know that God sees us and that all of His thoughts towards us are good. God wants to rescue you from you. He longs to gently turn your face towards Him and tell you, "You are more than enough." Let your heart speak to Him.

MIRROR, MIRROR, WHAT DO YOU SEE?

Mirror, mirror what do you see?

What do you see when I look at me?

Do you see a fierce warrior walking in victory?

Or a defeated soul living in misery?

Mirror, mirror what do you see?

What do you see when I look at me?

Do you see a wounded woman falling down?

Or do you see a royal daughter standing and fixing her crown?

Mirror, mirror what do you see?

What do you see when I look at me?

Do you see regret and deferred dreams?

Or do you see creativity flowing like rivers and streams?

Mirror, mirror what do you see?

What do you see when I look at me?

Do you see oppression, depression, bondage and chains?

Or do you see successes, triumphs and gains?

Mirror, mirror what do you see?

What do you see when I look at me?

Do you see the guilt and shame I despise?

Or do see the apple of His eyes?

Mirror, mirror what do you see?

What do you see when I look at me?

Do you see me as the villain in my life's play?

Is it the things I think or the words I say?

Mirror, mirror help me to see,

God's love when I see me!

Tojuan W. Minus

October 25, 2024

WORDS TO REMEMBER

- **Accepted** - generally approved; usually regarded as normal.

- **Affirmation** – solemn declaration of acceptance and recognition as God's own daughter.

- **Apple** - the center or pupil of the eye that expands and contracts through which light passes.

- **Chosen** - having been selected as the best or most appropriate.

- **Condemnation** - strong censure; disapprobation; reproof.

- **Elect** – picked out; a person or persons chosen by God, especially for favor or salvation.

- **Father** - Paternal affection, protectiveness, responsibility, etc.

- **Forsake** – to leave, loose, to be deserted, to let us loose, abandon.

- **Loved** - held in deep affection; cherished.

- **Orphan** - to deprive of parents or a parent through death.

- **Powerful** - having or exerting great force, authority, or influence; mighty.

- **Precious** – of high price or great value and worth; beloved.

- **Restore** - to bring back into existence, use, or the like; reestablish. to bring back to a former state.

- **Season** - a set time, appointed time.

- **Set Free** - discharged, liberated, pardoned.

- **Vindicate** - justify, prove correct or absolve from blame.

- **Workmanship** – that which is made.

This is my daughter in

whom I am well pleased.

HOW TO USE THE JOURNAL

God has affirmed you as His daughter and He is not changing His mind about you. This journal is to serve as a guide to direct, or in some cases, redirect your focus on what the Bible has to say about you and how God sees you.

Write and color in this journal at your own pace, in any order. Let this journal serve as tool to help you become your authentic self. It can be a resource to draw you closer to God and process His love for you through His lens of love. God knows everything you've done, yet His thoughts toward you are always loving. Girl, you're not so far gone that God cannot rescue you. He saw your bad decisions, heard every cuss word you spoke, saw all the rage and the vindictiveness in your head, yet He says, "I love you."

What's In Part I?

In Part One, there are five different affirmations using the acronym A.P.P.L.E.:

- Accepted – "I am accepted."

- Precious – "I am precious."

- Powerful – "I am powerful."

- Loved – "I am loved."

- Elect – "I am God's elect."

All five affirmations have scriptures and writing prompts that can serve as your one-on-one time with the Father. Take all the time you need for this journey. Just don't get stuck. If the tears come, let them flow, that is an indication of healing taking place. If the laughter comes, laugh out loud, laughter will be medicine to your soul. If remorse comes, forgive yourself.

What's In Part II?

Girl, it is time to embrace everything about you and let the Lord order your path to greatness. I believe as you search the scriptures, God will reveal even more to you. In Part II, I have provided a series of scriptures for you to research and ponder. Your missteps and anything you thought disqualified you to be in His presence was actually factored in before you were formed in your mother's womb. Sometimes we don't know what we don't know. Girl, God sees you and loves you madly. He sees you thriving and fulfilling purpose as the A.P.P.L.E. of His eye.

CONTENTS

Girl, He Sees You

PART I - WHO AM I IN CHRIST?

I HEARD HIM CALLING

Who has saved us and called us with a holy calling, not according to our works, but according to His own purpose and

grace which was given to us in Christ Jesus before time began,

II Timothy 1:9

As a child, I played Marco Polo with my friends at the public pool. When I was "It," I'd stand in the water, close my eyes, and call out "Marco." The other players responded with "Polo." My goal as "It" was to swim to a person and tag them. While playing, my friends could swim to a different location in the water and I didn't know because my eyes were closed. If I suspected that a player was out of the water, I could shout, "Fish out of water." If I was right, and someone was out of the water, they replaced me as the "It" and the game continued.

This childhood game came to mind as I pondered God calling me to Him. Instead of "Marco," I heard a gentle voice on the inside of me saying my name. Just like little boy Prophet Samuel in the Bible, I didn't know it was God's voice. So, when I heard my name, I tried to escape the call. I didn't even respond with "Polo" because I wanted to live my life on my terms. I heard Him call me again, "Tojuan" and I still didn't say "Polo." I didn't want to get tagged. I wanted to do what I thought Tojuan was big and bad enough to do. Even though my decisions were leading me to heartbreak and despair, I was not going to be one of those Bible toting folks I had seen.

After a while, I heard God call, "Tojuan," again. I knew I was a fish out water and I let God tag me. I was tired of swimming around a pool of anger, heartache and hurt.

Do you hear Him calling you? Are you afraid to answer? I understand if you are pondering. If you are independent and used to taking care of business on your own, it may not be easy to surrender to God's call. It requires trusting every second, minute, and hour of your life to His care, which can be scary for some people. It was scary for me. I was scared to open my heart and let God in. I was afraid He wouldn't like what He saw. I was 22 years old, for me it was easier to run. I look back now and say, "Why did I wait so long?" Some may think that that was too young, but I wish I had let Him tag me sooner. Why, you may ask… because He was what I was looking for all along. God was calling me because He wanted me to know why I was alive. I didn't know who I was, let alone my purpose.

My sweet surrender to God's call came on February 2, 1988. A friend who had answered His call for herself asked me to watch a video called, *Rock and Roll: A search for God*. I watched the video and realized that if I continued on the road I was on, I would end up eternally lost like those in the video. I finally surrendered and said, "Yes, Lord, here I am." When I did, I felt a loving warmth come over me unlike anything I had felt before.

Just as it had been when I played Marco Polo as a child, God tagged me, and I was it. Not only that, I was His.

THE APPLE OF GOD'S EYE

I believe every woman and girl has an image of their Prince Charming. You know, the great Love of their life, the one who sweeps her off her feet and takes her to the land of happily ever after. When you think of this Lover…what image comes to your mind? Is he tall, dark and handsome? Is he muscular? Is he an adventurous wealthy tycoon who lavishes you with the finer things of life? When your Prince Charming looks at you, do you get lost in his eyes and every one of your heart aches and pains melts into nothingness? When he hugs you, does the strength of his embrace comfort you and all your fears go away? Do you feel like you can conquer any challenge because you're by his side? Does he anticipate your every need and satisfy you completely? Does he celebrate you always?

When I think about my Lover, I'm very aware of how He looks at me and what He thinks about me. He wrote it in a Book for the world to see. My Lover, God, says that I am the apple of His eye in Psalm 17:8. My Lover sees every part me. He has known me from my beginning and continually celebrates my becoming. He gently calls my name and says, "Daughter, you are altogether lovely."

The apple is the pupil or the center of the eye. It is the sensitive, protective part of the eye. The pupil allows light to reflect in and out of the eye. My Lover's light reflects through me, and I am secure in His love. My Lover can't take His eyes off me. His joy and presence strengthen me. Because His eyes are always on me, He knows everything I've done, yet He says, "Come closer so I can love you more." His love transcends my past mistakes and failures. His love celebrates my accomplishments and edges me towards greatness because He is my greatest cheerleader.

This is how God sees us. He wants us to know this truth. Many times, we think we can't approach Him because of things we've done, but this is not the case. God wants us to run to Him. I can relate it to you through sharing about the time God taught me about roses. At one time I gave roses out to "forgotten" mothers in the community. I went to women's shelters, nursing homes, hair salons, and apartment complexes to hand roses to mothers. I noticed their physical reaction when receiving the rose from me in the form of oohs, aahs, smiles, and even tears. I asked God, "Why do women respond to getting flowers with such joy?"

As I pondered, God asked me, "What is a rose, Tojuan?"

Of course, I responded, "It's a flower."

He asked me again, "What is a rose, Tojuan?"

I knew I was thinking too literally, so I pondered the question. As I looked at the roses, I said, "A rose is your Word manifested. You spoke everything into existence."

He said, "You answered well." Then God explained, "When you were handing out the roses the women were receiving My Word. They were receiving the beauty and love that is in My Word. They were experiencing the softer side of Me."

We are living in a society where some are telling women we have to be hard, independent, or need to take charge and not take anything from a man. God is saying, "Receive My softer side. It's okay for you to be soft." Sometimes because of guilt, shame, and feelings of unworthiness, we think God is mad at us, however, that is not the case, He wants us to experience His tenderness.

In this journal, I want you to discover the softer side of God and how He sees you. God has a soft side and He has tremendous, unmatched power. He knows that you want to be:

- Affirmed, Accepted,

- Treated as a Precious jewel,

- Celebrated for your strength and Power,

- Unconditionally Loved, and

- Feel as though you are the only chosen, Elect one in her Lover's eye.

God is the ultimate Lover of your soul, and He longs for you to know that you are the A.P.P.L.E. of His eye.

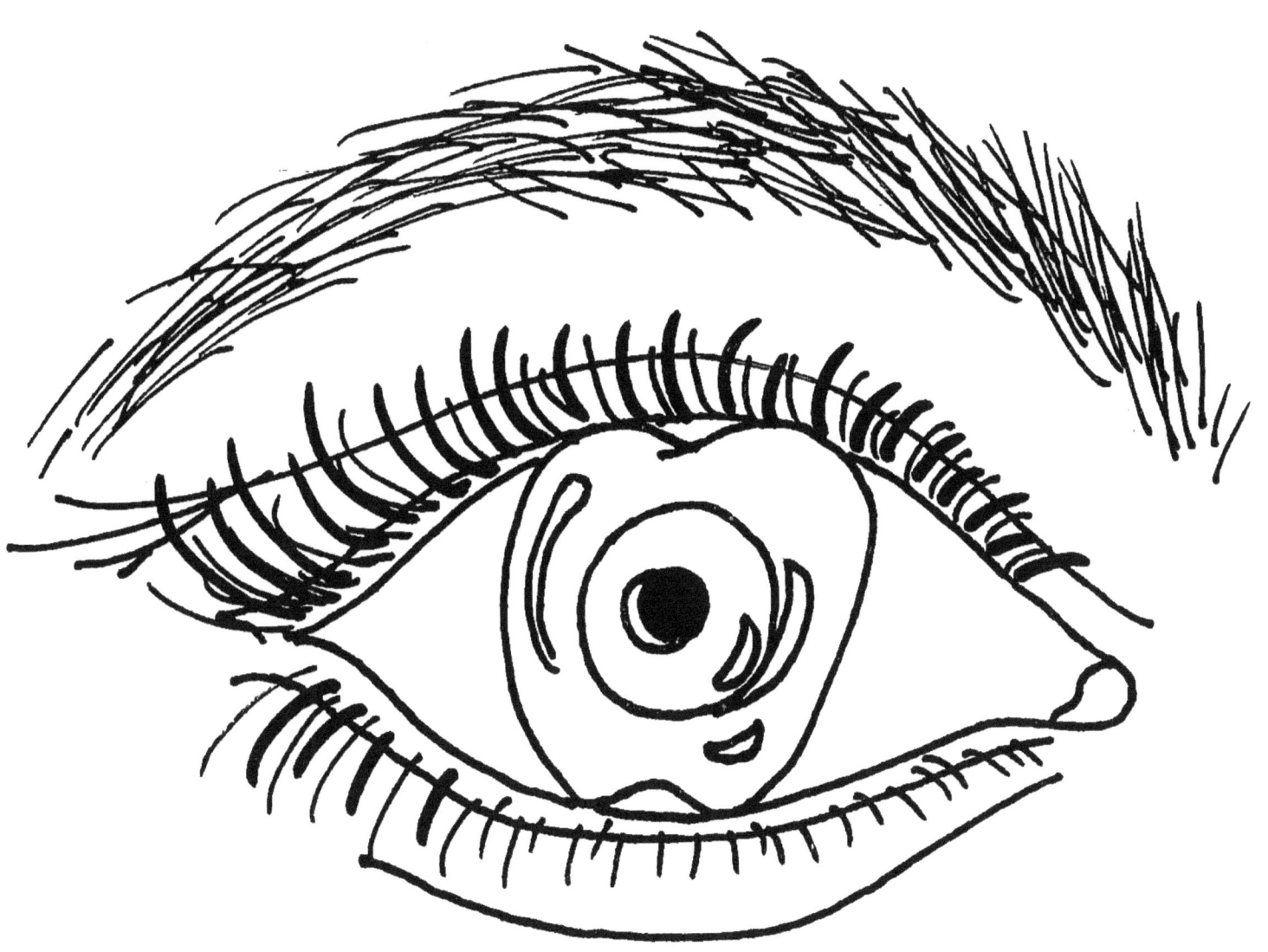

AFFIRMATION #1 - I AM ACCEPTED.

I AM ACCEPTED IN THE BELOVED

To the praise of the glory of His grace, by which He made us accepted in the Beloved.

Ephesians 1:6

Have you ever received a gift from someone, but you never opened it? Sometimes that is how people are with Jesus, He is a gift, but you must accept and open the gift. God says, "You are gifts to Me and I accept you." Some other words for accepted are: welcomed, approved, confirmed, chosen, preferred, established and received.

God welcomes you into His presence.

God's approval of you is sure.

God confirmed His love for you before you loved Him, He loved you first.

God chose you before you chose Him.

God prefers you as His Beloved.

God wants you to be established in Him.

God has accepted you just as you are.

God receives you as His daughter.

Replace the word "accepted" with a synonym listed on the previous page and write about it:

_____

_____

_____

_____

_____

_____

_____

_____

_____

_____

_____

_____

_____

_____

_____

_____

I HAVE A FATHER

A father of the fatherless, and a judge of the widows, is God in his holy habitation.

Psalm 68:5

I once read a childhood book about a bird trying to find his momma. The bird went all around town asking everything that moved, "Are you my momma?" Finally, the bird was able to connect with his momma.

It has been said that children are nurtured by their mothers, but find identity and purpose as they pattern themselves after their fathers. This becomes problematic if the father is not in the child's life for whatever reason, be it death, divorce, or by choice. When the father is absent, children can start to look for their identities in the wrong places. In the same way as the little bird was looking for his momma, some women start looking at other men to define who they are and how they should conduct their lives.

The internal cry of some women is, "Are you my father? What is my purpose?" Fathers teach daughters how men should treat them. A good father teaches his daughter to know her worth and value it. Even when natural fathers are not present, God says, "I'm a Father to the fatherless." Girl, God created you. He says, "I know who you are and what you are to do. I'm always here."

I have discovered that my relationship with my natural father has affected my relationship with God. My natural father and Heavenly Father are:

_____

_____

_____

_____

_____

_____

_____

_____

_____

_____

_____

_____

_____

_____

_____

_____

I AM SET FREE

Then said Jesus to those Jews which believed on him, If ye continue in my word, then are ye my disciples indeed;

And ye shall know the truth, and the truth shall make you free.

John 8:31-32

Imagine being in a prison cell and all the walls around you are made of 10-inch-thick cement. Imagine screaming and no one hears you. You're crying for help, and no one responds to you because no one hears your cries. Similar to that scenario, many people walk around silently screaming and hoping someone will hear them. Guess what? God knows your inner thoughts. He knows about your silent screams and sees them in your thoughts. He says, "Hold fast to Me and learn My truths." God's truths have the power to cut through the concrete and noise in your mind. His truth makes you free as you stay connected to Him.

The reality is, you are what you think, and you respond to life accordingly. Situations in your past can make you feel guilt and shame. When you keep reliving all of your past mistakes in your mind, you keep your minds in a self-imposed prison. Girl, we are all guilty of making mistakes. Have you accidentally spilled a red pop and it splattered on someone's white blouse? I have. Ask for forgiveness and make the situation right as best as you can. Don't replay your mistakes because each replay adds a layer of concrete around your mind. You will begin to think, "I am a mistake," instead of, "I made a mistake." God wants to set you free from everything you believed disqualified you because of your life's situations. He wants you to know who you are in Him. Open the door of your heart and let Him in.

What non-truths about myself are keeping me imprisoned? What do I want to be set free from this week? Write and talk to the One who opens prison doors and breaks through cement walls.

_____

_____

_____

_____

_____

_____

_____

_____

_____

_____

_____

_____

_____

_____

_____

_____

I AM VINDICATED

Vindicate me, O Lord my God, according to Your righteousness;

And let them not rejoice over me.

Psalm 35:24 (NKJV)

Have you been wronged and wanted to plead your case? Did you want to obtain, "Street Justice?" We're living in times where it's normal to "match energy" with others. Sometimes matching energy can escalate into unfortunate circumstances. It can cause you to act out of your normal character. I want to encourage you to set your mind on maintaining your peace. God waits until the cool of the day to vindicate His children. Maintain your peace. Stay connected to Him. He's got you! God can vindicate you, and you don't have to retaliate!

The word "Vindicate" means to justify, prove correct, or absolve from blame. Our God is the Master Vindicator. Oftentimes, He uses the concept of time to vindicate you. Time is the greatest vindicator, and it can literary clear your name. Who wants others to speak ill of them; people of integrity want to be believed.

Jesus was mocked by people who didn't understand His purpose, yet He didn't respond. He didn't get into a tit-for-tat conversation with His accusers. His accusers beat Him and hung Him on a cross to die because Jesus said He was the King of the Jews. Three days later, God vindicated Him. God vindicated Jesus with many crowns and established Him as King of all Kings for eternity. Is there a situation where you want to tell your side of the story? Trust God's way of doing it.

I will maintain my peace and stay connected to Him. He's got me. God vindicated me . . .

_____

_____

_____

_____

_____

_____

_____

_____

_____

_____

_____

_____

_____

_____

_____

_____

_____

I AM NOT FORSAKEN

I will never leave you nor forsake you.

Hebrews 13:5

Girl, sometimes people will forsake you. It could be over a simple disagreement, or someone moves to a different city, state, or country. Seasons change, people change, and people leave. God will never leave you, nor will He forget. you. The term "ride or die friend" takes on a whole new meaning when it's God. Girl, He sees you! It's assuring to know that God is not fickle with His feelings toward us. He decided before the foundation of the earth, "I will always be here for my daughters." He is not leaving you. Many may have chosen to leave Him, but He will never leave you. That should be comforting to know.

Many of people have carried wounds of rejection because their worth was not valued. Some have seen your value to them but did not value you. You were accepted as long as it benefited them. They used your gifts, wasted your time and resources, and then when they were done, they dismissed you out of their lives. Girl, I know the pain of being abandoned by someone you loved deeply. Their rejection can make you question your purpose. They may have crushed your soul for a season, and you may have even sat in a pit of remorse for a while. But guess who was sitting with you, the God who sees all. He stayed right there with you and helped you process the pain of rejection and betrayal. He said, "Where she goes, I go. I am not leaving her in this situation." You know the strength you had to get up? That was Him, lifting you. Spend this week forgiving those who despitefully used you.

I was forsaken, yet God intervened:

_____

_____

_____

_____

_____

_____

_____

_____

_____

_____

_____

_____

_____

_____

_____

_____

_____

_____

AFFIRMATION #2: I AM PRECIOUS.

I AM PRECIOUS TO GOD AND HONORED BY HIM

Since you were precious in My sight, You have been honored, And I have loved you.

Isaiah 43:4 (NKJV)

Did your grandmother or someone you know have fine China? Great care was taken to preserve the beauty of the ornate plates, saucers and tea cups. Those dishes were not ordinary and your grandmother cherished the special, precious, and uncommon dishes, only bringing them out for special occasions. The sentimental value of the China was evident in how your grandmother cared for the delicate porcelain. They were washed and towel dried in a certain way, and positioned on the table perfectly, their beauty used to enhance the tablescape.

Unlike your grandmother, God celebrates your specialness, strength, and uniqueness daily. Just like a regal tablescape with each dish, glass and flatware having a unique spot, you have a unique place in God's heart. He knows your value. Just like a beautiful ruby or fine piece of China, He sees you as extraordinary, rare, and one-of-a kind. You are precious to God and He honors you with a loving presentation.

You are like an exquisite jewel, with enduring worth and matchless beauty. Jewels are categorized as precious when they possess an exceptional rarity, durability, and beauty. You are cherished by God as a jewel because you are His beloved daughter. When you speak of something being precious to you, it speaks of something of great value and worth. When God says you are precious in His sight, He is saying, "Daughter, I hold you in high regard. You are valuable."

What does it feel like knowing I am precious to God:

_____

_____

_____

_____

_____

_____

_____

_____

_____

_____

_____

_____

_____

_____

_____

_____

_____

_____

_____

I AM NOT AN ORPHAN

I am adopted by God.

Ephesians 1:5

Back when I was growing up, there were more households with mothers and fathers raising children together. As a child, my normal was not having my father in the home. We lived in the same city, but we didn't interact much. Although my father was alive, I felt deprived and orphaned because I was left out of his daily interactions. Children teased me because I didn't have a daddy.

The pain and the shame of being fatherless followed me into adulthood. I wondered, "Why wasn't I good enough to have my father around? What is wrong with me?" I discovered that I was never an orphan because my heavenly Father was always there with me, I just had to learn to tap into His presence.

In life you can feel left out or deprived. like the popular character, Rudolph the Red Nosed Reindeer. In the story, a group of reindeer deprived him of attention, acceptance and community. But Rudolph always had good standing with Santa Claus. He may have been left out of the reindeer games, but he was not left out of the family.

You may feel like an orphan and outcast, but you're never left out of God's family. You are accepted into His family. God sees you as His child. He decided to adopt you into His family long before you knew Him. God longs for a family to love and He loves you.

Have I ever felt orphaned or left out?

_____

_____

_____

_____

_____

_____

_____

_____

_____

_____

_____

_____

_____

_____

_____

_____

_____

_____

_____

I AM BORN AGAIN INTO NEW LIFE

Being born again, not of corruptible seed, but of incorruptible, by the word of God,

which liveth and abideth forever

1 Peter 1:23

In darkness, in the stillness of your mother's womb, He knitted you perfectly. In the darkness, He said, "Let there be light," and the light came. As you wandered aimlessly, in despair, looking for direction, He wooed you into a new light, a new birth. Not a return into your mother's womb, but a spiritual awakening, you were born again as a Daughter of the King.

Black is the mysterious moody color that must be a stable in every woman's wardrobe. The little black dress, lacy black lingerie, stilettos, a leather jacket, and a Coach purse. Some women need black mascara, lip liner, and a black smoky eye, also. Black is the colorless color that enhances all things. Some say black is the color that accents all other colors; making those colors stand out. You know the combinations: Black plus gold, blue, or pink. Black plus green, orange, red, white, purple, and silver. Yes, there is a saying, "Black as me."

Some people believe that black is the mixture of all colors. My experience says, "Not so fast. The mixture of all colors produces a murky brown, black stands alone. Black is supreme." How can one fully appreciate the stars without black skies? How can you appreciate light without darkness? Go, to and fro, enhancing the colors of the world. Share His love and hope to young, old, rich, and poor, to the enlightened, and the uninformed. Share the Good News of salvation and new life, let them see Him who made all colors.

What does it mean to me to have a new life in Him:

_____

_____

_____

_____

_____

_____

_____

_____

_____

_____

_____

_____

_____

_____

_____

_____

_____

_____

I HAVE SEASONS

To everything there is a season, and a time to every purpose under the heaven.

He hath made everything beautiful in His time.

Ecclesiastes 3: 1, 11

"I see seasons everywhere." This line from a song rings true in our lives. I once found myself in a season where I had to pivot to care for a family member. I wondered how to find balance between care, creativity, community, and my Call. Everything has a season, but there is one thing that will not change, no matter what season it is. I am a Daughter of the King. That is my position and ultimate FLEX. Everything else is subject to change. We can find ourselves in what I call a "free fall" season.

I once dreamed that I was walking up the steps of a marble columned mansion. Beautiful women of all shapes and colors were wearing flowing white gowns. Some had gold shoes and others wore silver shoes. I asked God, "Who are these women?" He responded, "My daughters." As I turned in a circle, looking at everything, I noticed a door in the corner. I wondered why there was a framed wooden door in the midst of the paleaceous palace. I gingerly walked across the marble floors and swung the door open. I stood at the threshold and looked inside, observing a storm with high winds, rain, and water everywhere. Then I heard the gentle voice of the Lord say, "Step in there."

I protested, but took a deep breath and stepped over the threshold, into the storm. It felt like I was falling, but I wasn't afraid; I felt peace in the eye of the storm. I felt my body floating. I woke up and said, "WHOA! What was that?" It was my free fall into fully trusting the embrace of my Father.

What do I need to do in order to give God my complete trust?

_____

_____

_____

_____

_____

_____

_____

_____

_____

_____

_____

_____

_____

_____

_____

_____

_____

_____

I AM NOT FORGOTTEN

When my father and my mother forsake me, then the Lord will take me up.

Psalm 27:10

Have you ever been out shopping and saw a person you used to interact with all the time, but couldn't remember the person's name? I'm guilty. When that happens, I usually stand there and have a nice conversation thinking, "*What is her name?*" Out of embarrassment, neither of us asked for the other's name. LOL! I've learned from this kind of situation that constant interaction keeps people connected.

Girl, God doesn't forget your name like that. Isn't that good to know? Do you know that if you're not talking to God or reading your Word, He still remembers you. God is like the friend, that no matter how long it has been since you talked, rejoices when you engage in conversation. Just like when you talk with your girlfriend, it's back and forth, open and honest, raw and real, you can dialog with God the same way. He welcomes the time and longs for those conversations with you.

Girl, God knows everything about you. He has not forgotten anything about you. Remember, you are the apple of His eye. You are always in the forefront of His thoughts, forever before Him. He is always available for You.

Has it been a while since you had a chat with God? Go ahead and start the conversation, take a deep breath, and just say, "Hello, it's me." He is lovingly waiting to pick up where you left off your last conversation.

My prayers for people I have "forgotten" . . .

_____

_____

_____

_____

_____

_____

_____

_____

_____

_____

_____

_____

_____

_____

_____

_____

_____

_____

AFFIRMATION #3 - I AM POWERFUL.

THE POWER TO THINK IN NEW WAYS

Casting down imaginations and every high thing that exalted itself against the knowledge of God and bringing into captivity every thought to the obedience of Christ.

2 Corinthians 10:5

Self-talk is vital to your purpose and destiny. Girl, what's your self-talk like?

Words carry power and God sees it as "high thing" or barrier that blocks your destiny when you say, or think something contrary to His Truth. He wants you to demolish negative thoughts and replace them with His Word. You're probably thinking, "How do I do that? I have been thinking this way for so long." Guess what, bad thoughts can be replaced with good thoughts.

Girl, I spent years feeling unworthy and self-conscious about my appearance. I saw others as more successful, more prosperous, even more beautiful. I believed the lies the enemy was suggesting about me. My journey of casting down imaginations started with asking God to forgive me for not loving what He loves. I would stand in the mirror and look at myself and say, "I love what God loves, and He loves me." I replaced negative thoughts about myself with God's Truth. I visualized an image in my mind of a vacuum cleaner removing negative thoughts and leaving behind God's Truth.

The truth is, you are going to make mistakes, but you are not a mistake. You are loved by your Heavenly Father. That love is not based on what you do, but on who you are. Spend this week casting down imaginations, thoughts, judgements, and hostile reasonings that are contrary to God's Truth. Ask God to show the areas that made you agree with the lies of the enemy.

What do I believe that is contrary to God's truth?

_____

_____

_____

_____

_____

_____

_____

_____

_____

_____

_____

_____

_____

_____

_____

_____

_____

_____

What do I believe that is contrary to God's truth?

I AM THE LIGHT

Ye are the light of the world. A city that is set on a hill cannot be hid.

Matthew 5:14

Darkness is the absence of light. Light is a source of illumination. In Genesis 1:3, God said, "Let there be light." Girl, God says you are the light of the world. Remember, darkness was upon the face of the deep (Genesis 1:2). In Genesis 1:3, the Bible says, let there be light of life and light of prosperity. In John 8:12, Jesus said, "I am the light of the world." His presence dispels darkness in our life, darkness in our understanding, and darkness in our spirit. Before Jesus left to go back to the Father, He gave us a charge to be the light of the world.

Girl, you are His light in the earth because His spirit is living in you. Let your light shine bright in the darkness. Where there is darkness in your life whether it be at work, school or in your family, SHINE!!! Your light can dispel all that is dark around you.

I am the Light . . .

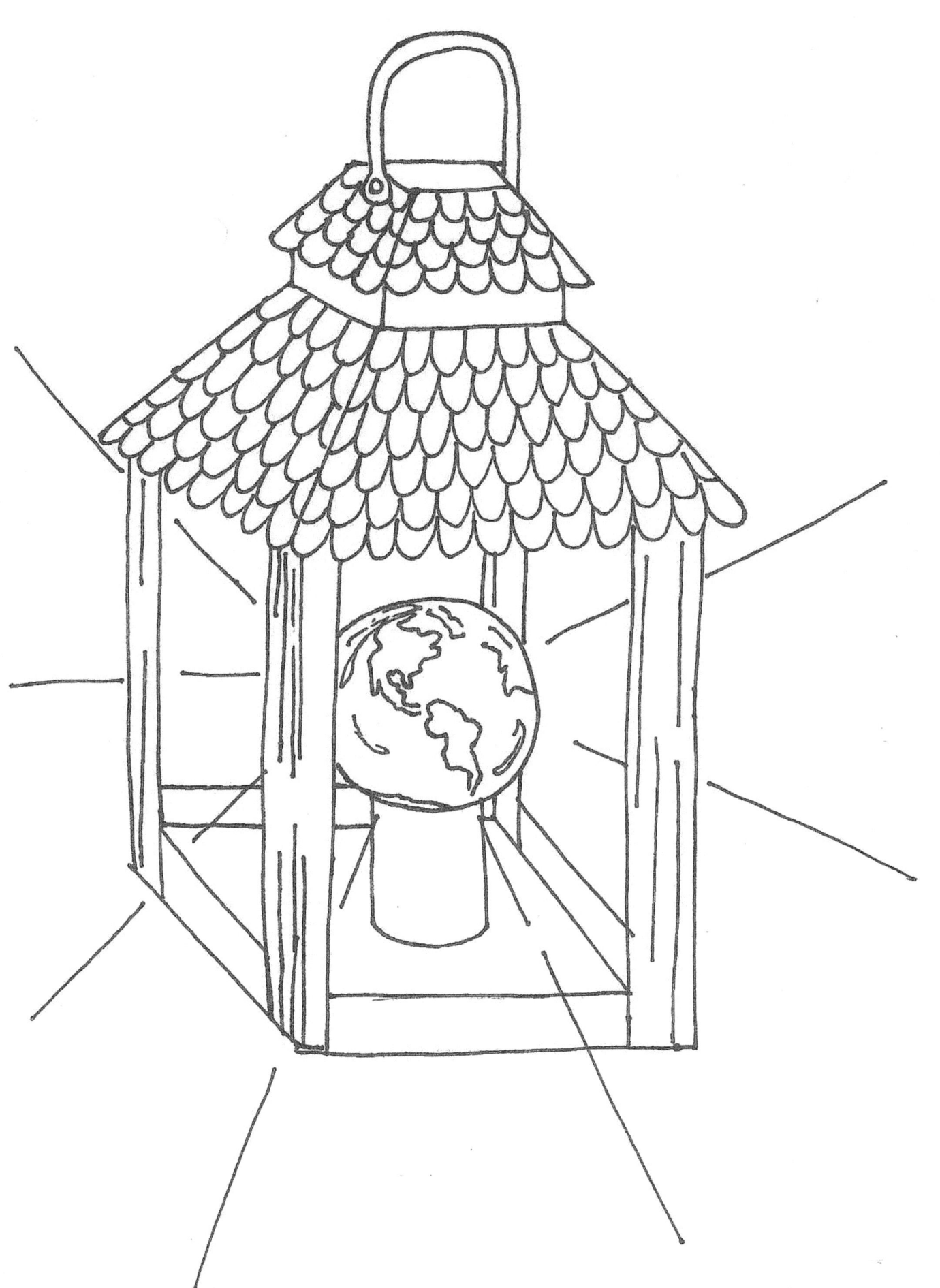

I AM THE SALT

"You are the salt of the earth; but if the salt loses its flavor, how shall it be seasoned? It is then good for nothing but to be thrown out and trampled underfoot by men.

Matthew 5:13

Have you ever eaten something that tasted as though it had no flavor? When that happens, most people add a little salt to the dish to help with the flavor. Every good chef knows that salt is the secret ingredient to all cooking preparations. Salt enhances sweet and savory dishes. It's the flavor bomb that dances on your tongue, which pleasures the pallet. Salt is the finishing touch, the secret sauce, and the goodness in all matters of cooking.

Salt is also a preservative that can extend the life of a substance. Salt prevents decay. Epsom salt, known for its therapeutic properties as a detoxifier, exfoliator, muscle relaxer, and stress reliever, helps reduce inflammation.

Girl pause; God calls you the SALT of the earth! You bring the flavor. You are the enhancement. You bring joy, preservation, and healing to the earth. Your presence on the earth makes life challenges more palatable to many. Colossians 4:6 teaches that God wants the words you speak to be "seasoned" as with salt, graciousness, and peace.

Girl, STAY SALTY!!!

Who needs my salt?

_____

_____

_____

_____

_____

_____

_____

_____

_____

_____

_____

_____

_____

_____

_____

I BRING GOD PLEASURE IN MY PROSPERITY

Let them shout for joy and be glad, Who favor my righteous cause; And let them say continually, "Let the Lord be magnified, Who has pleasure in the prosperity of His servant."

Psalm 35:27 (NKJV)

Imagine having a cheerleader for eternity. God wants you to prosper, be successful, and thrive. He delights, has a high degree of enjoyment in your prosperity. He wants you to do well, flourish, bloom, and yield increase on every side. Prosperity is more than having money in your bank account. It's important, but God wants more for you. In every area of your life, He wants you to be successful. 3 John 2 says that God wants you to prosper and be in good health even as your soul prospers.

Prosperity in every area of your life may require you to realign your mind, emotions, and health to this truth. Your mind is the key to success. How you think determines how you approach life. If you think you can, you will, and vice versa. Believing that you cannot do something may impact your ability to achieve it. Sometimes your prayer has to be, "Today, Lord, I change my mind." Notice I didn't encourage you to pray for the Lord to change your mind. You must change your own mind. To change your mind, you must renew it with God's Word. Search the scriptures and see what God has to say about you. This journal is a start, but there is so much more God has to say about you.

Did you know you have the power to make God smile? He is magnified in the earth when you PROSPER and THRIVE! I dare you to go BE GREAT TODAY!

I bring God pleasure in my prosperity when . . .

_____

_____

_____

_____

_____

_____

_____

_____

_____

_____

_____

_____

_____

_____

_____

_____

_____

_____

I AM FORGIVEN

In Him we have redemption through His blood, the forgiveness of sins, according to the riches of His grace.

Ephesians 1:7

My brother and I fought a lot as children. Momma made us say that we were sorry, when we really weren't. Likewise, when my son and oldest daughter got into spats, I'd make them apologize. Saying "I'm sorry" sometimes made my daughter angrier about the situation because she was absolutely not sorry for her actions. Years later, while teaching in a classroom, when two children got into a scuffle, intending to hurt each other, my assistant separated them and told them to apologize. There was no remorse between the two children.

To be sorry is to feel regret, compassion, sympathy, or pity. When one offers an apology, they express regret, remorse or sorrow for having insulted, failed, injured, or done wrong to another. As I matured in my walk with God, I started to understand that forgiveness is a word that would have been appropriate in each situation I mentioned. When you forgive, you give up all claims, or cancel an ineptness. When we ask for forgiveness with a pure heart, He is faithful and just to forgive us. (1 John 1:9) Accept His forgiveness today.

Have you ever asked someone to forgive you? They'd say, "I forgive you, but I won't forget what you did." Their mouths say one thing, but heart says another. God isn't like that. When He forgives us, it is as if the offense never happened. He is not like some people; He forgives and won't hold a negative attitude in His heart towards you. He gives up His claim to imprison you for wrongs you committed. Isn't that powerful and reassuring? His love towards you transcends your mistakes.

I am forgiven . . .

_____

_____

_____

_____

_____

_____

_____

_____

_____

_____

_____

_____

_____

_____

_____

_____

_____

_____

AFFIRMATION #4: I AM LOVED.

I AM LOVED

I have loved you with an everlasting love. Therefore, with lovingkindness I have drawn you.

Jeremiah 31:3 (NKJV)

God is love. You cannot comprehend love fully without God because His very essence is Love. He is love motivated and love driven. While we were yet sinners, Love found its way to us. God gave His best to us, His most precious gift, a piece of Himself. He gave up His divine nature to live as a human. He gave up everything for a relationship with us and laid down His divinity. "What's love got to do with it???" It's a cliché. It's a song. It's a movie. But what's love got to do with your relationship with God? EVERYTHING!!

God's love for us moved Him to give His only begotten Son as a sacrifice for our sins. His love was unconditional. In other words, we didn't have to perform to deserve it. We didn't have to be "good" to receive it. His love says, "I love you in your entirety: good, bad, your shameful, your doubtful, your wishy-washy condition." His love says, "I love you even when you don't love Me."

Girl, God's unconditional love for you is settled and will never change. He woos you to experience His love even when you think you don't deserve it. His love is everlasting and a sure thing.

I am loved with an everlasting love . . .

_____

_____

_____

_____

_____

_____

_____

_____

_____

_____

_____

_____

_____

_____

_____

_____

_____

_____

LOVE, 4 WAYS

The Bible outlines four distinct types of love. Implementing love in daily life can lead to stronger, more fulfilling relationships. You can reflect the multifaceted nature of love as depicted in the Bible, ultimately bringing individuals closer to living a life that mirrors God's love.

- **Agape** – Agape love woos us to experience God's love even when we don't feel like we deserve it. This is God's love for humanity and is considered the highest form of love. It is often described as selfless, sacrificial, and unconditional. This is the glue that keeps us connected to God. It's a love that surpasses physical touch although we can feel His love. Agape love says:
  - "I love you in your entirety, good, bad, shameful, doubtful, wishy-washy condition."
  - "I love you, even when you don't love Me or even like Me."
  - Agape love says you are worth loving (unconditional and sacrificial love) and represents the unconditional and sacrificial love that God has for us, It calls us to embody God's love towards others, setting the foundation for how love can transform and enrich our lives.

- **Eros** – Eros love focuses on the passionate and romantic aspect of love reserved for marriage, illustrating its role in deepening the connection between married couples.

- **Storge** - Storge love emphasizes the natural and instinctual love within families, showcasing the importance of familial bonds and the support system they provide.

- **Philia** – Philia love stresses the importance of friendship and the deep, mutual bonds that can exist between individuals, highlighting how these relationships are gifts to be cherished.

How do I define love . . .

_____

_____

_____

_____

_____

_____

_____

_____

_____

_____

_____

_____

_____

_____

_____

_____

_____

_____

God's love for me is . . .

_____

_____

_____

_____

_____

_____

_____

_____

_____

_____

_____

_____

_____

_____

_____

_____

_____

_____

My love for my family is . . .

_____

_____

_____

_____

_____

_____

_____

_____

_____

_____

_____

_____

_____

_____

_____

_____

_____

_____

_____

I love unconditionally . . .

_____

_____

_____

_____

_____

_____

_____

_____

_____

_____

_____

_____

_____

_____

_____

_____

_____

What I need in a friend . . .

_____

_____

_____

_____

_____

_____

_____

_____

_____

_____

_____

_____

_____

_____

_____

_____

_____

_____

_____

_____

I AM FREE FROM CONDEMNATION

There is therefore now no condemnation to them which are Christ Jesus,

who walk not after the flesh, but after the Spirit.

Romans 8:1

Everyone has done something they are not proud of. Have you ever replayed an unfortunate event in your mind? Did you think, "What was I thinking about when I did that? Why did I do that?" You are in great company. In the Bible, the Apostle Paul pondered, "Why do I do what I don't want to do, and I don't do what I ought to do?"

If you muster too long in this thought process, guilt and shame can dominate your thoughts. Guilt is when you feel bad for doing something, and shame is feeling that *you* are inherently bad. God does not want you to live in either of those realities, nor does He want you to walk around condemning yourself. God's intent is not to give you a damnatory sentence for your errors. He sent His Son to set you free from sin. Accepting the free gift of salvation gives you access to walk in freedom from the guilt of your past and confidence for a prosperous future.

God is not sitting in heaven looking to punish you for every wrong. He is a loving Father. He wants you to run towards Him and say, "Father I messed up. Forgive me." He is faithful and just to forgive. Then you must forgive yourself. Don't condemn yourself because God is not condemning you. Change your mind and forget those things which are behind you. In other words, God is not keeping count, neither should you.

I am free from condemnation . . .

_____

_____

_____

_____

_____

_____

_____

_____

_____

_____

_____

_____

_____

_____

_____

_____

MY SLEEP IS SWEET

When you lie down, you will not be afraid; Yes, you will lie down and your sleep will be sweet.

Proverbs 3:24 (NKJV)

I never liked horror movies as a child. If I snuck and saw something scary, I would be up all night, thinking about the scene, or that the "boogey man" was going to get me. I'd ask Momma if I could sleep with her. Sometimes she would say yes and sometimes she would say no. If she said no, I mastered the art of sneaking into her bed because I wanted to feel safe and secure. Girl, I can laugh about it now, but back then, I was scared. As an adult, I still don't like scary movies.

Sometimes life can have you tossing and turning. It can be like the scary scene of a horror movie playing over and over in your head. You can lay in bed overthinking choices, overprocessing decisions, and just feeling overwhelmed. You wonder about bills, your job, your kids, spouse if you are married, and even the future. Our world can be challenging or as people say, Life be "life-ing."

You have a Father who never sleeps or slumbers. He wants you to rest. Isn't that reassuring? You can have sweet sleep because He is handling business for His children 24 hours a day, seven days a week. He created your body to rest, not stress. When you are stressing, tossing, or turning, deep down you don't think God can handle your life situation. Or you may be wide awake at night, trying to figure out how God will handle it. God is in control of everything. He's got this.

Girl, let God handle it, go to sleep.

In order to have sweet sleep I must . . .

_____

_____

_____

_____

_____

_____

_____

_____

_____

_____

_____

_____

_____

_____

_____

_____

_____

_____

I AM RESTORED

He restoreth my soul: he leadeth me in the paths of righteousness for his name's sake.

Psalm 23:3

I like watching decorating shows where rundown homes are brought back to their original state. It's been said one person's trash is another person's treasure. In a similar way, God wants to restore you to your original purpose. Sin, life and circumstances can cause you to neglect your purpose and destiny.

The Lord says He will restore your soul. Your emotions, will, and mind make up your soul. Lack of alignment in your soul can cause you to view God and people through unhealed emotions. God says He will realign your soul according to how He originally created you. Isn't that good to know? He is the Master Restorer of souls. Think about it, in the Bible the physical body is likened to a house. Sometimes people do not properly care for their house. They eat the wrong things and clutter their thoughts with wrong thinking.

Do you maintain the upkeep of your house? Are there cobwebs in the corner of your soul that you have not addressed?

What needs to be restored in you? Is it hope? Is it joy? Is it confidence? Is it strength? Talk to your Father today and develop a restoration plan for your success. He loves you and wants your house to be the best on the block.

I am restored . . .

AFFIRMATION #5: I AM GOD'S ELECT.

I AM GOD'S ELECT

12 Put on therefore, as the elect of God, holy and beloved, bowels of mercies, kindness,

humbleness of mind, meekness, longsuffering;

Colossians 3:12

In America, every four years we exercise our right to vote for our President and other government officials. We, the people, pick who we want to represent us as a nation. We give these elected people the right to speak on our behalf, make decisions on our behalf, and to lead us as a nation. This is the definition of a Republic. However, in the Kingdom of God, things are different. We don't vote for God, He is the Supreme Ruler over everyone and everything in the universe. God is Sovereign and His vote is the only one that counts in His Kingdom. His vote is for you; He elects, or chooses you.

Just as we expect certain character traits in our government officials, God expects certain traits to be evident in us. We expect our government officials to be honest, trustworthy, compassionate, and strong decision makers. As God-elected officials in the earth, there are character expectations for this position. The fruit, or character of the spirit is love, joy, peace, patience, kindness, goodness, faith, meekness and self-control. These are the character traits God wants you to put on, like a dress. These qualities aid you in being effective as His Elect. Do you want to succeed in every situation? Let these things be your wardrobe of choice at all times. Girl, the clothing of gossip, drama, negative thinking and bad attitude must be replaced. It's time for a new dress. Take the time to search your character clothing and see what pieces you need to add. God wants you styled with the character of His spirit.

Because I am the elect of God . . .

_____

_____

_____

_____

_____

_____

_____

_____

_____

_____

_____

_____

_____

_____

_____

_____

_____

_____

I AM CHOSEN

But ye are a chosen generation, a royal priesthood, a holy nation, a peculiar people…

1 Peter 2:9

Were you ever in a position when you had to be picked for a team? Did your heart pound during the process? Did you wonder if you would be chosen? Were you chosen first? Did it feel good? Was there a time when you were picked last? Did it make you feel sad?

Guess what? God chose you before you chose Him. He loved you first. He thought you were the best choice. Sometimes, you focus on what you were not chosen for and think something is wrong with you. Did you know not being chosen can be God protecting you? If the guy you just knew was going to be your husband chose another you felt some type of way. You later found out, although he looked attractive to you, he lacked the character to love you as you desired. Then God revealed who He chose for you and you thank God for protecting your heart.

Spend this week writing about times in your life when you were chosen and accomplished something great. Write about when you felt like you should have been chosen for something and another was selected such as job promotion, a sports team, or a university admission.

Because I am chosen in Christ . . .

I AM GOD'S WORKMANSHIP

For we are his workmanship, created in Christ Jesus unto good works,

which God hath before ordained that we should walk in them.

Ephesians 2:10

As an early childhood educator, I encouraged creativity when I worked with children. It never failed that the children would compare their art to the other children's. Comparison kills creativity. If they saw something that "appeared" to be more advanced, the comments were pretty much the same. "I don't like mine. Hers looks better." I often said, "There is nothing wrong with your work because you made it that way. You made it exactly how it should be because it's your unique work."

In that same way, we are God's workmanship. Girl, you are a uniquely crafted work of art from God. The artistry that is you cannot be compared to anyone else. You were thought out in the mind of God. God did not mess up with you. He did not say, "I should have made her like somebody else." Each of us was lovingly and joyfully made. When you compare yourself to others, your uniqueness gets lost.

Think about the millions of dollars spent on plastic surgery. People try to "fix" something, so they are what others define as beautiful. Some even try to look like someone else. The earth has many flowers, trees, and animals, but the most treasured workmanship God created was you. Every detail of your being was on purpose. Spend time this week focusing on you as God's artistic expression. How does that make you feel? Is it comforting? Is it strange?

I believe that I am God's workmanship . . .

_____

_____

_____

_____

_____

_____

_____

_____

_____

_____

_____

_____

_____

_____

_____

_____

_____

I AM AN AMBASSADOR

I am an ambassador for Christ.

2 Corinthians 5:20

An ambassador is a high-ranking diplomat who represents a country in another nation. Did you know that where ambassadors reside in foreign countries are considered jurisdictions of their countries of origin? So, if I am an ambassador in France, then the house I live in would be considered United States' land.

Think about it, as an ambassador for Christ you represent Kingdom concerns. You speak on heaven's behalf. When you share the gospel of the Kingdom, you offer heavenly diplomacy to those who have no hope. Girl, God has entrusted you to represent Him on earth as a Kingdom Ambassador. You establish heaven on earth with your actions and deeds. When people see you, they see and understand the Kingdom of God. He has faith in you to do the job! You bring God's love, peace, patience, justice, and hope from your heavenly country to earth.

Girl, represent well!

I am an ambassador for Christ . . .

_____

_____

_____

_____

_____

_____

_____

_____

_____

_____

_____

_____

_____

_____

_____

_____

_____

_____

_____

I AM A JOINT HEIR WITH CHRIST

And if children, then heirs; heirs of God: and joint-heirs with Christ: if so be that we suffer with him, that we may also be glorified together.

Roman 8:17

Years ago, I watched a documentary on the British monarchy. In the British monarchy everyone and everything was subject to the Queen. She was the sovereign one. If she had a need, it was instantly given to her. In the documentary, it was established who would receive her inheritance upon her demise. It was also established what heir would sit on her throne.

This documentary helped me understand Kingdom concepts. In Psalm 24, the scripture declares that the earth is the Lord's, the world, and all that dwell therein. God is the Sovereign of the Universe and His heir is Jesus (Hebrews 1:2).

The Bible declares that you are a joint heir or co-heir with Christ. God accepted you into the family. You are a child of God (Romans 8:16) with rights and privileges that come with being a Daughter of the King. You are His royal heir (Galatians 4:7), and He has an inheritance for you. The inheritance comes through your acceptance by faith of the free gift of salvation through Jesus Christ. Yes, for some, life has had challenges and it has been hard. But your hope is in this, if you share in this world the sufferings of life with Jesus, you will also share in the glory to come. Your inheritance is sure. You are an heir to the promises, blessings, power, and authority that is in Jesus.

Girl, go get your inheritance!

I am a joint heir with Christ . . .

Girl, He Sees You

Part II: What Does God Say About Me?

I am God's child (His Daughter).

– John 1:12

_____

_____

_____

_____

_____

_____

_____

_____

_____

_____

_____

_____

_____

_____

_____

_____

_____

_____

I have access to the Father.

— Ephesians 2:18

_____

_____

_____

_____

_____

_____

_____

_____

_____

_____

_____

_____

_____

_____

_____

_____

_____

I am complete in Him.

— Colossians 2:10

_____

_____

_____

_____

_____

_____

_____

_____

_____

_____

_____

_____

_____

_____

_____

_____

_____

_____

_____

I am secure.

– Romans 8:38-39

_____

_____

_____

_____

_____

_____

_____

_____

_____

_____

_____

_____

_____

_____

_____

_____

_____

_____

_____

I can forgive others.

– Ephesians 4:32

_____

_____

_____

_____

_____

_____

_____

_____

_____

_____

_____

_____

_____

_____

_____

_____

_____

_____

I am the righteousness of God through Christ.

– 2 Corinthians 5:21

_____

_____

_____

_____

_____

_____

_____

_____

_____

_____

_____

_____

_____

_____

_____

_____

_____

_____

_____

_____

I am blessed when I obey His commands.

– Deuteronomy 28:1-14

I am washed, sanctified, and justified.

— 1 Corinthians 6:11

_____

_____

_____

_____

_____

_____

_____

_____

_____

_____

_____

_____

_____

_____

_____

_____

_____

_____

_____

_____

I am victorious.

– Revelation 21:7

_____

_____

_____

_____

_____

_____

_____

_____

_____

_____

_____

_____

_____

_____

_____

_____

_____

_____

I am more than a conqueror.

– Romans 8:37

_____

_____

_____

_____

_____

_____

_____

_____

_____

_____

_____

_____

_____

_____

_____

_____

_____

_____

_____

I have a sound mind.

– 2 Timothy 1:7

I am strong in the Lord.

– Ephesians 6:10

_____

_____

_____

_____

_____

_____

_____

_____

_____

_____

_____

_____

_____

_____

_____

_____

_____

_____

_____

I am comforted.

– Isaiah 66:13

_____

_____

_____

_____

_____

_____

_____

_____

_____

_____

_____

_____

_____

_____

_____

_____

_____

_____

_____

_____

I am a first fruit of His creation.

– James 1:18.

_____

_____

_____

_____

_____

_____

_____

_____

_____

_____

_____

_____

_____

_____

_____

_____

_____

_____

_____

I am a saint.

– Romans 1:7

I have God's anointing and Spirit to teach me.

– 1 John 2:27

_____

_____

_____

_____

_____

_____

_____

_____

_____

_____

_____

_____

_____

_____

_____

_____

_____

_____

_____

I am crucified with Christ.

– Galatians 2:20

_____

_____

_____

_____

_____

_____

_____

_____

_____

_____

_____

_____

_____

_____

_____

_____

_____

I am transformed and my mind is renewed.

– Romans 12:2

_____

_____

_____

_____

_____

_____

_____

_____

_____

_____

_____

_____

_____

_____

_____

_____

_____

_____

I am formed and set apart.

– Jeremiah 1:5

I am sealed with the promised Holy Spirit.

– Ephesians 1:13

_____

_____

_____

_____

_____

_____

_____

_____

_____

_____

_____

_____

_____

_____

_____

_____

_____

_____

I am created by God in the womb.

– Psalm 139:13-16

_____

_____

_____

_____

_____

_____

_____

_____

_____

_____

_____

_____

_____

_____

_____

_____

_____

_____

I am adopted as His child.

– Ephesians 1:5

I am not afraid.

– Hebrews 13:6

I am a new creature in Christ.

— 2 Corinthians 5:17

_____

_____

_____

_____

_____

_____

_____

_____

_____

_____

_____

_____

_____

_____

_____

_____

_____

_____

_____

I have redemption through Christ.

– Ephesians 1:7

I have strength because of His joy.

– Nehemiah 8:10

_____

_____

_____

_____

_____

_____

_____

_____

_____

_____

_____

_____

_____

_____

_____

_____

_____

_____

_____

I have purpose.

– Ephesians 1:9

I am His disciple.

– John 13:15

_____

_____

_____

_____

_____

_____

_____

_____

_____

_____

_____

_____

_____

_____

_____

_____

_____

_____

_____

I am not in want.

– Philippians 4:19

_____

_____

_____

_____

_____

_____

_____

_____

_____

_____

_____

_____

_____

_____

_____

_____

_____

_____

I follow God because I know His voice.

– John 10:3-5

Nothing can separate me from the love of God.

– Romans 8:38-39

I am born of God and I overcome.

– I John 5:4

I have an abundant life through Christ.

– John 10:10

_\

I can approach God with freedom and confidence.

– Ephesians 3:12

I am a holy temple.

– 1 Corinthian 6:19

I am promised eternal life.

– John 6:47

_____

_____

_____

_____

_____

_____

_____

_____

_____

_____

_____

_____

_____

_____

_____

_____

_____

_____

_____

I am growing.

– Colossians 2:7

I am a minister of reconciliation.

— 2 Corinthians 5: 17-20

I am called of God by name.

– Isaiah. 49:1

I am healed by the wounds of Jesus.

— 1 Peter 2:24

I think in new ways.

– Philippians 4:8-9

_____

_____

_____

_____

_____

_____

_____

_____

_____

_____

_____

_____

_____

_____

_____

_____

_____

I have a royal heritage.

– 1 Peter 2:9

_____

_____

_____

_____

_____

_____

_____

_____

_____

_____

_____

_____

_____

_____

_____

_____

_____

_____

I am qualified to share in His inheritance.

– Colossians 1:12

_____

_____

_____

_____

_____

_____

_____

_____

_____

_____

_____

_____

_____

_____

_____

_____

_____

_____

I am engraved in the palms of God's hands.

– Isaiah 49:16

_____

_____

_____

_____

_____

_____

_____

_____

_____

_____

_____

_____

_____

_____

_____

_____

_____

_____

_____

_____

I have the mind of Christ.

– 1 Corinthians 2:16

I am at peace with my enemies when I please the Lord.

– Proverbs 16:7

_____

_____

_____

_____

_____

_____

_____

_____

_____

_____

_____

_____

_____

_____

_____

_____

I am shielded when I put my trust in God.

– Proverbs 30:5

_____

_____

_____

_____

_____

_____

_____

_____

_____

_____

_____

_____

_____

_____

_____

_____

_____

I have God's unfailing love.

– Psalm 32:10

_____

_____

_____

_____

_____

_____

_____

_____

_____

_____

_____

_____

_____

_____

_____

_____

_____

_____

I have a Greater One in me than he who is in the world.

– 1 John 4:4

I am delivered from the power of darkness.

– Colossians 1:13

I always triumph in Christ.

– 2 Corinthians 2:14

I can do all things through Christ.

– Philippians 4:13

GOD WILL DELIGHT IN MY SUCCESS

I have a goal to:

Date To Accomplish: _____

GOD WILL DELIGHT IN MY SUCCESS

I have a goal to:

_____

_____

_____

_____

_____

Date To Accomplish: _____

GOD WILL DELIGHT IN
MY SUCCESS

I have a goal to:

Date To Accomplish: _____